GRADE

4

The 2007 & 2008 Syllabus should be read for details of requirements, especially those for scales, aural tests and sight-reading. Attention should be paid to the Special Notices, where warning is given of any changes.

The syllabus is obtainable online at www.abrsm.org, from music retailers or from the Services Department, The Associated Board of the Royal Schools of Music, 24 Portland Place, London W1B 1LU, United Kingdom (please send a stamped addressed C5 (162mm x 229mm) envelope).

In exam centres outside the UK, information and syllabuses may be obtained from the Local Representative.

CONTENTS

Where appropriate, pieces in this volume have been checked with original source material and edited as necessary for instructional purposes. Fingering, phrasing, pedalling, metronome marks and the editorial realization of ornaments (where given) are for guidance only; they are not comprehensive or obligatory.

Editor for the Associated Board: **Richard Jones**

DO NOT
PHOTOCOPY
© MUSIC

Alternative pieces for this grade

© 2006 by The Associated Board of the Royal Schools of Music

No part of this publication may be copied or reproduced in any form or by any means without the prior permission of the publisher.

Music origination by Barnes Music Engraving Ltd
Cover by Økvik Design
Printed in England by Headley Brothers Ltd,
The Invicta Press, Ashford, Kent

Prelude in F

BWV 927

from *Clavier-Büchlein vor Wilhelm Friedemann Bach*

J. S. BACH

DO NOT PHOTOCOPY © MUSIC

This prelude is drawn from a little oblong manuscript book that Bach began on 22 January 1720 and devoted to the instruction in keyboard playing and composition of his eldest son, then only nine years old. Already Wilhelm Friedemann was being taught equality of the two hands: though the LH starts with accompanying chords, it takes over the theme itself in bb. 3–4. Quavers might be lightly detached. Dynamics are editorial suggestions only.

Source: *Clavier-Büchlein vor Wilhelm Friedemann Bach*, Library of the School of Music, Yale University, Connecticut, USA

© 1988 by The Associated Board of the Royal Schools of Music
Adapted from J. S. Bach: *A Little Keyboard Book*, edited by Richard Jones (ABRSM Publishing)

AB 3146

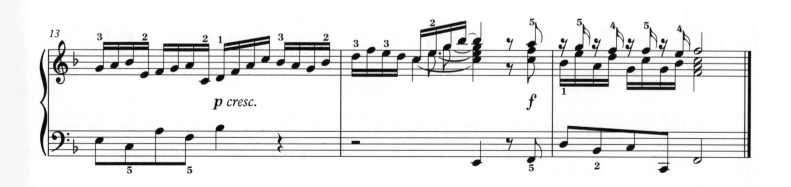

4

A:2

Air

No. 17 from *24 Progressive Lessons*, Op. 37

Edited by
Howard Ferguson

HOOK

DO NOT
PHOTOCOPY
© MUSIC

James Hook (1746–1827) was precociously gifted as a child. He played concertos in his native town of Norwich at the age of six and had composed a ballad opera by the age of eight. He spent most of his adult life as an organist in London, at Marylebone Gardens and later at Vauxhall Gardens. In this Air, all dynamics are editorial suggestions only.

Source: *Guida di musica, Being a Complete Book of Instructions for Beginners on the Harpsichord or Piano Forte…to which is added 24 Progressive Lessons*, Op. 37 (London: J. Preston, 1785)

© 1982 by The Associated Board of the Royal Schools of Music

Reproduced from *A Keyboard Anthology*, Third Series, Book 2, edited by Howard Ferguson (ABRSM Publishing)

A:3

Preludio

from Suite No. 1 in B minor,
Sonate d'intavolatura, Part 2

ZIPOLI

Domenico Zipoli (1688–1726), a pupil of A. Scarlatti and Pasquini, was appointed organist of the Jesuit church in Rome in 1715. Two years later, however, he settled in Córdoba, Argentina, where he studied for the priesthood but died before he could be ordained. This prelude is drawn from Zipoli's *Sonate d'intavolatura* of 1716, a collection of organ and harpsichord pieces that became very popular due to its appealing, melodious style. All dynamics are editorial suggestions only. The ornaments in bb. 22–5 are original; all the others are editorial.

Sources: *Sonate d'intavolatura, parte seconda*, Op. 1 (Rome, 1716); *Six Suits of Italian Lessons*, Op. 1 (London, 1725)

© 2006 by The Associated Board of the Royal Schools of Music

DO NOT
PHOTOCOPY
© MUSIC

El fantasma

No. 8 from *Cuentos de la juventud*, Op. 1

Edited by
Thomas A. Johnson

GRANADOS

Enrique Granados (1867–1916) was essentially self-taught as a composer. From 1890 onwards he established a reputation as a concert pianist, and in 1901 founded his own music school, the Academia Granados, in his native town of Barcelona. His musical style fuses elements of the 19th-century Romantic tradition with the idioms of Spanish folk music. The *Cuentos de la juventud* (Stories of the Young), from which 'El fantasma' (The Ghost) is drawn, was his first published collection of keyboard music.

© 1985 by The Associated Board of the Royal Schools of Music
Reproduced from Granados: *Cuentos de la juventud*, Op. 1, edited by Thomas A. Johnson (ABRSM Publishing)

Cattle-Call

No. 1 from *19 Norwegian Folksongs*, Op. 66

GRIEG

The Norwegian composer Edvard Grieg (1843–1907) became acquainted with L. M. Lindeman's collection of folk music *Older and Newer Mountain Melodies* in 1869, and thereafter often made use of Norwegian folk tunes in his music. 'Cattle-Call' is drawn from his *19 Norwegian Folksongs*, Op. 66, of 1897. In bb. 1–2, the tie between the middle notes of the lower-stave chord has been added by analogy with bb. 17–18.
Source: *19 hidtil utrykte norske folkeviser*, Op. 66 (Leipzig, 1897)

© 2006 by The Associated Board of the Royal Schools of Music

Petits bateaux sur l'eau

DO NOT PHOTOCOPY © MUSIC

Edited by
Lionel Salter

SANDRÉ

Petits bateaux sur l'eau Little Boats on the Water

Gustave Sandré (1843–1916) was director of the Nancy Conservatoire in eastern France, where Florent Schmitt was one of his pupils. Most of his compositions were published around 1900 as supplements to the magazine *L'illustration*.

© 1990 by The Associated Board of the Royal Schools of Music
Reproduced from *More Romantic Pieces for Piano*, Book 2, edited by Lionel Salter (ABRSM Publishing)

DO NOT
PHOTOCOPY
© MUSIC

C:1

Alarm

from *On the Great Liner*

BJELINSKI

Allegro ♩ = 144

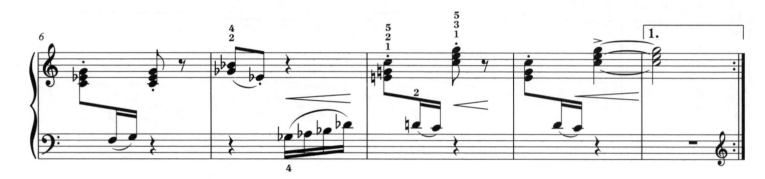

Bruno Bjelinski (1909–92) was a Croatian composer who studied law at Zagreb University, then music at the conservatory in the same city. He taught for over 30 years (1945–77) at the Zagreb Academy of Music. A suitable tempo for 'Alarm' in the exam would be ♩ = *c*.112.

© 1966 by Musikverlage Hans Gerig, Köln

© 1980 assigned to Breitkopf & Härtel, Wiesbaden. All enquiries for this piece apart from the exams should be addressed to Breitkopf & Härtel, Walkmühlstraße 52, 65195 Wiesbaden, Germany.

Bop Goes the Weasel

No. 4 from *Jazz-It: Twinkle, Twinkle Jazzy Star*

DO NOT PHOTOCOPY © MUSIC

BILL READDY

Bill Readdy (b. 1953, London) is a teacher, pianist and composer with a particular interest in jazz piano. His collection *Jazz-It: Twinkle, Twinkle Jazzy Star* contains 15 easy, jazzy arrangements of well-known European children's songs. In this piece, dotted-quaver, semiquaver rhythms should be swung; the quavers in b. 22 should be played straight.

© 2004 Schott & Co. Ltd
Reproduced by permission. All enquiries for this piece apart from the exams should be addressed to Schott & Co. Ltd, 48 Great Marlborough Street, London W1F 7BB.

At the Bottom of My Garden

No. 1 from *Practical Guide*, Album 7

DO NOT PHOTOCOPY © MUSIC

VILLA-LOBOS

Poco moderato [♩ = *c*.80]

Heitor Villa-Lobos (1887–1959) was the outstanding Brazilian composer of the 20th century. Immensely prolific, he united the techniques of contemporary European art music with elements of the folk and popular music of his native country. 'No fundo do meu quintal' – to give this piece its Portuguese title – is drawn from his *Guia prático*, a large collection of pieces based on popular Brazilian children's songs.

Copyright © 1947 by Mercury Music Corporation
Copyright Renewed. International Copyright Secured. All Rights Reserved. Used with Permission. All enquiries for this piece apart from the exams should be addressed to Carl Fischer, LLC, 65 Bleecker Street, New York, NY 10012, USA.